Original title:
Life's Purpose in a Nut Shell

Copyright © 2025 Creative Arts Management OÜ
All rights reserved.

Author: Fiona Harrington
ISBN HARDBACK: 978-1-80566-134-4
ISBN PAPERBACK: 978-1-80566-429-1

The Heart's Compass

My heart said go, and off I flew,
But my legs were stuck like glue!
A dance of dreams, a twist of fate,
But doesn't walking feel like bait?

I chase my hopes like kids at play,
But tripping up just makes my day!
With every step, I laugh and grin,
Why not fall, if I can win?

A Symphony of Choices

I ponder choices, big and small,
Like picking snacks at a carnival!
Ice cream or popcorn, such a strife,
Now that's a dilemma in real life!

Shall I wear blue, or maybe pink?
Each choice I make, I stop to think.
A symphony of chaos rings,
Should I follow what the birdie sings?

Fleeting Shadows

Shadows chase me when I'm out,
A game of tags, there's no doubt!
They dance and play just like me,
But can shadows be truly free?

I run around, they start to flee,
Maybe they're just shy, you see!
If they giggle when I call,
Are they shadows, or friends after all?

The Quest for Clarity

I sought clear signs like a puzzled knave,
But all I got was a confused wave!
Should I follow the map, or take a chance?
Or join that squirrel for a wild dance?

I squint and ponder with a sigh,
Why do questions pile up so high?
But with each laugh, I feel it fade,
Clarity, dear friend, is often delayed!

Chasing Light

In the morning sun, we trip and fall,
Chasing shadows that seem so tall.
With coffee spills and laughter loud,
We waltz around, a silly crowd.

Like moths drawn to a buzzing light,
We dance and twirl, oh what a sight!
Each stumble, giggle, that wild dash,
Is part of the fun, a silly splash.

Garden of Possibilities

In a garden where dreams take flight,
We plant silly seeds, oh what a sight!
With watering cans full of cheer,
We giggle at weeds, and shed a tear.

The carrots smile, the tomatoes sing,
While daisies play hopscotch in a ring.
Who knew a sprout could do a jig?
Life's quirks grow big in this rosy gig.

Embracing the Unknown

We wear blindfolds and hop around,
Playing leapfrog over unknown ground.
With goofy grins and hearts so bold,
We leap into adventures told.

The unknown's a jester with a sly wink,
It tickles our sides and makes us think.
In every twist and turn we find,
A funny mystery, a treasure bind.

Waves of Serenity

On the beach, we ride the tide,
With beach balls bouncing and hearts open wide.
We surf on laughter, glide on glee,
As sea foam tickles our toes with spree.

The waves whisper secrets, playful and bright,
While seagulls caw with sheer delight.
In a splash of joy, we find our way,
Surfing the comedy of each day.

Echoing Through the Cosmos

In the vastness, I shout so loud,
Yet the echo laughs, forms a crowd.
Stars are winking, I seem to roam,
Searching for meaning, I call it home.

Riding comets, I sip on stars,
Pondering life from Mars to bars.
With a twinkle, it just seems clear,
The purpose could be making beer!

The Journey of a Single Step

One step forward, oh what a thrill,
Tripped on my shoelace, down I spill.
Yet with laughter, I'll rise again,
This journey's better with a bit of pain.

With every stumble, a giggle comes,
Life's a dance, just sway and hum.
Step by step, I'll find my groove,
Waltzing with chaos makes me move!

Petals of Perseverance

In a garden where hopes bloom bright,
Petals drop, yet I'm still in flight.
A bee buzzes, what's the fuss?
Pollinating dreams, no need to rush.

With a chuckle, I chase the sun,
Even weeds think they're just as fun.
Who knew growing could be a game?
I'll plant my jokes, then stake my claim!

The Tangle of Purpose

I tangled my thoughts like messy hair,
Purpose? Ha! It vanished in the air.
Chasing squirrels, I lose my track,
But who needs plans? Just laugh and snack!

With ropes of dreams, I tie a bow,
All the knots just help me grow.
So if you trip on this winding track,
Join the circus, let's never look back!

The Melody of Existence

In the music of waking, a dance is begun,
With socks on the wrong feet, we laugh and we run.
Each day is a concert with outfits untamed,
Conducting our dreams, though the cat is unnamed.

Bouncing through chaos, we sing out of tune,
With pancakes for dinner and spoons as our flute.
We juggle our wishes, like balls made of cheer,
In the rhythm of laughter, we know we are near.

Sparks of Inspiration

A light bulb flickers, but where did it go?
Ideas fly wildly, like popcorn in flow.
We surf on our thoughts, like waves made of cheese,
Embracing the nonsense, we do what we please.

With crayons and doodles, we sketch our grand schemes,
Turning napkin sketches to gold-plated dreams.
In bursts of creativity, giggles ignite,
For humor is fuel to our flights of delight.

The Touch of Time

Time's tick-tock is silly, like shoes on a cat,
It dances in circles, a dizzying spat.
We chase after minutes, like ice cream on cones,
While counting our blessings, and losing our phones.

Granny tells stories of moments that flew,
With waffles for wisdom and tales that ensue.
Embracing the chaos, we find hidden gems,
For clocks may tick loudly, but laughter transcends.

A Breath of Meaning

In the air we exhale, a giggle takes flight,
With purpose as fluffy as clouds made of light.
We wander through nonsense, seeking the point,
While wearing our hats that are overly blunt.

Each breath is a whisper, a tickle, a wink,
In searching for meaning, we find time to blink.
We tumble through life with a grin and a tease,
So let's brew our fun, oh, let's stir up some ease.

Voices in the Silence

In the quiet, thoughts parade,
Like squirrels with nuts, unafraid.
Chasing dreams in a jigsaw mess,
Hoping stress is just a guess.

Jokes on fate, as we all trip,
Over socks that liked to skip.
Dancing through the mundane haze,
Finding laughter in the craze.

The Trail Blazed by Hearts.

With hearts as compasses, we roam,
Building castles made of foam.
Finding joy by jumping high,
While wearing shoes that bloop and sigh.

Each stumble tells a tale or two,
Of mixed up dance steps, just for you.
With every hop, a spark ignites,
Unruly laughter, bold delights.

The Whisper of Existence

A whisper floats on coffee steam,
With missed puns that make us gleam.
We sip and ponder on the quest,
Is breakfast truly the best fest?

Chocolate cakes in a sunny split,
Are moments that make minutes sit.
In the chaos, we bless the blocks,
Chasing quirks like playful socks.

Seeds of Tomorrow

Planting seeds in mismatched shoes,
For future blooms and funky hues.
We giggle at the growing chore,
While wishing we just bought some more.

In gardens wild where weeds conspire,
We laugh at dreams that never tire.
Through tangled paths, we skip and play,
Embracing all the ups and sway.

Bridges Beyond Tomorrow

Why chase the fleeting time,
When socks dance without a rhyme?
Goals like balloons, they pop and fly,
While I just eat another pie.

I built a bridge with silly dreams,
It wobbles more than it seems.
Yet, laughter echoes far and wide,
As I stumble through this ride.

Whispered Affirmations

In the mirror, I declare,
'You're fabulous, but don't go bare!'
Each morning holds a goofy grace,
As I trip over my shoelace.

With coffee beans and dreams in tow,
I whisper plans, then let them go.
For life's a dance of flops and spins,
Just as I start, the chaos begins.

The Orchard of Hope

There's an orchard where smiles bloom,
With fruit that chases away the gloom.
But watch out for the bees that buzz,
They sneak up fast, as if they were fuzz.

In the shade, I dream and stew,
While munching on an apple or two.
Hope's sweet nectar, tart or bright,
Makes me giggle with delight.

The Art of Letting Go

Letting go is quite the feat,
Like losing socks, can't find the pair neat.
I throw my worries in the air,
Then trip over them, unaware.

With every laugh, I shed a load,
My heart's a comedy, on this road.
As I dance, a little too free,
I find that laughter's key for me.

Glimmers of Infinity

In a world of socks unmatched,
We ponder why their pairs are scratched.
Chasing dreams like wild birds fly,
Laughing at the reasons why.

Underneath the moon's bright eye,
We carry on while time slips by.
Wishing for the perfect loaf,
Yet finding joy in burnt soft hope.

With frowns turned upside down, my friend,
We juggle life 'til the very end.
Swapping tales of silly tries,
Finding truth in goofy lies.

So here's to twists, to turns unplanned,
With rubber chickens close at hand.
The punchlines wrap our days so tight,
In giggles, we unlock the night.

The Sway of the Universe

The world spins round like a ballerina,
Wobbling dreams and double meaner.
We strut and fret, a comical mess,
In this cosmic play, we're all dressed less.

Like hamsters on wheels, we dash with flair,
While pondering how to shape our hair.
Chasing stars that twinkle above,
Wondering if they're symbols of love.

Kites caught in branches, they squeal and croon,
Singing sweet tunes to the light of the moon.
As we dance through the fog and the haze,
Laughter erupts, brightening the ways.

So here we sway, in this cosmic ride,
With mismatched socks and hearts open wide.
Embracing the quirks 'neath the big, vast dome,
In this wobbly ballet, we feel at home.

The Dance of Becoming

A jiggle here, a shuffle there,
We sway with grace or just with flair.
In the rhythm of coffee spills and laughs,
We question maps and other gaffes.

In a line for tacos, we find our crew,
Swapping stories, silly yet true.
With a twirl of fate and a sprinkle of luck,
We trip on shadows but never get stuck.

With jellybeans and the occasional pie,
We wonder aloud, "Why do we even try?"
Yet in chaos, we find hidden gems,
Bathtub symphonies and whimsical diadems.

So dance with glee on this strange earth stage,
Embrace the weird, let go of the cage.
As we shuffle through moments, never alone,
In the dance of becoming, we find our throne.

Cracks of Illumination

Through cracks in the sidewalk, wisdom spills,
Amidst scattered leaves and phantom thrills.
We trip over thoughts, lose our way,
Yet laughter guides us, come what may.

Each morning greets us with toast and jams,
While the cat plans world domination scams.
Peeking through windows with curious eyes,
We dodge the boredom, wear our disguise.

In kitchens full of dreams gone awry,
Mismatched ingredients dance and sigh.
From spaghetti mishaps to flour fights,
We find life's humor in the fateful bites.

So here's to the cracks that let the light,
Shine on our fails, brilliant and bright.
As laughter echoes in simple tunes,
We embrace the odd under dancing moons.

Echoes of the Heart

In the quest for bliss, we trip on our own shoe,
Chasing big dreams like it's a game of peek-a-boo.
We juggle job, hobbies, and perhaps a cat,
Is breakfast even important? Who knows? Not that!

Yet laughter spills out like a bubbling pot,
We dance through our chaos, embracing the plot.
With regrets marinated in yesterday's stew,
We leap into tomorrow, just trying to break through.

Take a cue from squirrels, with acorns in tow,
They stash away dreams, to nibble, then grow.
So here we are, in this circus of fun,
Happiness isn't a race, it's a pun under the sun.

So let's toast to the mess, raise our glasses with glee,
For life is a short play, so let's make it silly!
With echoes, we laugh, we sing till we're hoarse,
Navigating this journey, a very wild course.

The Canvas of Dreams

I dipped my brush in a puddle of hope,
Splattering laughter, like confetti on slope.
Each stroke a misstep, yet wildly it gleams,
Creating a masterpiece out of silly dreams.

With clouds made of marshmallows floating on high,
I painted the wishes I've tucked in the sky.
My palette is spicy, with colors that bite,
Every stroke uttering, 'Hey, isn't this right?'

I stand back in wonder, at my patchwork of fun,
It's stunningly jumbled, yet bright like the sun.
My friends all align, admiring the mess,
Claiming they knew I had talent, no less!

Yet in all this chaos, where is the framed art?
It's in the laughter shared, that warms every heart.
While critics may frown at my colors so rare,
I revel in joy, for my soul's canvas is bare.

Sunlight on the Journey

Strolling down sidewalks with shoes untied,
Waving at pigeons who look a bit fried.
Occasionally lost, as I look for the map,
But there's beauty in motion, like a bus with no cap.

With sunbeams as guides, I leap and I bound,
Each twist in the road brings a giggle profound.
Who needs the skyline? I've got daisies to smell,
They offer sweet wisdom, more than man can tell.

Oh, there's wisdom in laughter, it lightens the load,
Hopping like bunnies, we bounce down the road.
A soda can rolling becomes a new game,
Around every corner, it's never the same.

So here's to our journey, with sunshine ablaze,
To finding the funny in the maze of our days.
With a wink and a grin, let joy be our aim,
For we're all just a part of this wild, wacky game!

Fragments of Fulfillment

In a world made of puzzles, we search for the piece,
While chaos surrounds, we giggle, at least!
We dig through the cushions, it might be in there,
In the fur of the dog, or beneath the full chair.

Like wedding cake tiers, our moments stack high,
Each slice is a memory, oh my, oh my!
We toast to the victories, both big and quite small,
And dance like no one's there, just to stand tall.

We gather our fragments in bags labeled 'fun',
Confetti of laughter, before we are done.
With hearts full of echoes, we skip down the street,
Every stumble a step brings us closer to sweet.

So here's to the search, to the wild, silly quest,
For joys that are fleeting, but feel like a fest.
In the scramble for meaning, let's lift up our cheer,
For fulfillment can be found when we just disappear!

Whispers of Tomorrow

In the morning sun, we rise and shine,
Chasing dreams like cats at play,
Dodging worries, sipping wine,
Laughing at the silly fray.

Every moment's like a joke,
Wrapped in giggles, wrapped in cheer,
Like that time the chicken spoke,
Who knew clucks could spread such fear?

We juggle tasks like circus bears,
Honking horns, and leaving trails,
Dancing 'round our little cares,
Like mismatched socks and tales of snails.

At the end, we'll toast with glee,
With wobbly chairs and icing fun,
To years gone by, and used-to-be,
As we laugh until we're done.

The Essence of Being

What's the secret, they all ask?
As I munch on cookies, looking wise,
Maybe it's not too much of a task,
Just counting giggles, not the fries.

In the grand scheme of things, it seems,
We're but actors in a play,
Dreamers feeding silly dreams,
While we dance the night away.

The toaster pops, the coffee brews,
And still we wonder, what's the score?
It's all about the silly views,
And breaking bread with friends galore.

When the curtain drops, we'll sing,
With mismatched socks and peanut pie,
What a funny, glorious fling,
Life's a giggle, my oh my!

Seeds of Destiny

Planting seeds in goofy rows,
Water them with jokes and cheer,
Watch them grow with silly shows,
And dance around when they appear.

Each sprout whispers a funny tale,
Of squirrels debating donut holes,
With every leaf, we shan't derail,
As laughter fills our little souls.

If tomatoes wear a silly hat,
And carrots sing with a croaky voice,
Why not let the lettuce chat?
In this garden, we rejoice!

So let's dig in, unfurl our dreams,
With garden gnomes that cheer us on,
In the soil of what life seems,
It's all a game—let's have some fun!

Threads of Existence

Weaves of gold and frays of thread,
Stitched to stories, old and new,
Some tangled up, while others spread,
Like spaghetti tossed, just for you.

Each knot contains a hearty laugh,
Of blunders made and wonky turns,
In this fabric, we all craft,
With winks and nods, as the world learns.

Thread by thread, we weave our tale,
From giggles shared to candy bars,
We'll patch the rips and share a ale,
While dancing 'neath the fuzzy stars.

So here's to laughter, here's to fun,
To thread the needle, loud and bright,
In this adventure, we have won,
With every stitch, we take our flight!

The Tapestry of Being

In a world of endless threads,
We stitch our dreams with mismatched reds.
A pattern here, a knot held tight,
We giggle as we weave by night.

Each patch absurd, a tale to tell,
Like socks that somehow fit so well.
Laughter colors our woven fate,
Stitching joy, a stitch of fate.

Hummingbird's Flight

Zooming in with zippy glee,
A hummingbird sips nectar, whee!
With every flap, a whirlwind dance,
It's not just wings; it's pure romance.

Chasing blooms from pink to blue,
Who knew work could feel so new?
A sip of sweetness, buzz so bright,
In a flash, it takes flight!

The Alchemy of Now

Mix a pinch of joy with care,
A dash of whimsy, light as air.
Brew your moment, stir with flair,
Serve it warm, it's quite a dare!

A splash of laughter in the pot,
Add a twist, give it a shot.
In this cauldron, dreams collide,
Sip it slow, enjoy the ride!

Tides of Reflection

Waves rolling in, a playful tease,
Under sunlight, we float with ease.
Catch a wave, then get knocked down,
Laugh it off, don't wear a frown.

Mirrors of water, fair and bright,
Show us silly side in light.
We splash, we dance, we take the tide,
Savoring each comedic ride.

Reflections in a Pond

I looked into the pond today,
Saw my reflection swim away.
Thought I'd try to catch a fish,
But all I found was a muddy dish.

With every splash, I made a mess,
The fish just laughed, I must confess.
I pondered hard, what to do next,
Maybe a different thought to text.

The frogs croaked tales of lofty dreams,
While I pursued my silly schemes.
Yet in the ripples, wisdom gleamed,
Even the muck can be redeemed.

So here I sit, with fishy friends,
In laughter, my logic bends and bends.
A life in fun, a playful rhyme,
Reflecting joy, so light, so prime.

The Art of Becoming

They say to grow, don't be a fool,
But I still trip over my own stool.
Each great leap leads me to a fall,
Where's the art? I can't find it at all.

I try to sketch my grand design,
With crayons that work only half the time.
With doodles scattered, I stand bemused,
Still, I giggle at what I've produced.

A masterpiece of chaos, it seems,
Paint splatters become my wild dreams.
And in this mess, I start to see,
True beauty lies in sloppiness, whee!

So here's to growth, it's quite a blast,
With all my failures, I'm having a blast.
As I become, I laugh and play,
Embracing the wackiness of each day.

A Journey Within

To travel deep, I packed my bags,
With snacks and jokes, and silly tags.
But every step inside my head,
I found the couch where I was led.

I strolled through thoughts that made me grin,
While battling with my inner din.
Each twist and turn led me around,
Just to find, I was homebound.

I stumbled on some hidden fears,
And laughed with ghosts from bygone years.
Yet in the clutter, I found a clue,
A ticket stub labeled 'Just Be You.'

So here's my journey, filled with cheer,
With every laugh, I shed a tear.
In corners deep, I've learned to spin,
The funniest truth, it starts within.

The Colors of Aspiration

I painted dreams with colors bright,
Used neon pink and glow-in-the-night.
Yet when I looked, the canvas was bare,
It seems my brush had gone elsewhere.

I mixed and stirred with shades of stress,
End up wearing paint on my dress.
In wild strokes, I tried to define,
That big success, but fell out of line.

With every spatter, I found some glee,
Creating art no one's to see.
Yet in my heart, those colors pop,
Bright hues of hope that never stop.

So here I stand, splattered and bold,
With each wild stroke, my story's told.
In laughter's palette, I find my way,
Wearing my dreams in a playful display.

Doubts and Dreams

In a world of swirling thoughts,
I chase my dreams like runaway tots.
But doubts jump out, a sneaky crew,
Stealing my thunder, but what can I do?

I trip on wishes, fall on schemes,
While juggling my laughter and pie-filled dreams.
The path is wobbly, but oh, what a show,
With clowns and confetti, I'm never too slow!

I ponder questions, dance with jest,
Is my goal the big cheese or just a small fest?
With every detour, I chuckle and cheer,
Because the journey is nuts, but I'm still right here!

So here's to the madness, the ups and the downs,
Finding meaning with laughs, not frowns.
For in this circus of wonders, it's clear,
My purpose is giggles, and that's perfectly dear.

Notes from the Soul

In a mailbox of musings, I found a stray note,
It whispered sweet nonsense, like a goat on a boat.
"Dear soul," it said, "You're quite the fine mess,
But purpose is laughter, I must confess!"

A wink from my heart, like a fluttering kite,
Said, "Chase after giggles, and hold on tight!
Forget all the worries that stick to your shoe,
Your call is to chuckle, and that's how you grew!"

With melodies humming, I danced on my feet,
As ice cream and sunshine made life feel so sweet.
It's not about plans neatly drawn in a line,
But the crazy adventures and chocolate divine!

So I gather my notes, compose a fine tune,
Of tickles and hiccups beneath the bright moon.
With each silly scribble, the truth starts to unfold,
Life's melody's funny; it's a sight to behold!

The Secret of Your Compass

Oh compass of mine, with a needle so spry,
Where do you point when you're feeling sky-high?
I twist you and twirl you, like spaghetti on plates,
Searching for secrets while juggling with crates!

You say "north" with a wink and "east" with a grin,
But all my directions seem silly as sin.
I follow your lead with a hop and a skip,
But end up at places that make my heart skip!

The treasure I seek is a pot filled with glee,
Not gold or a mansion, but just being me.
So I'll dance with my compass, embrace every spin,
For the joy is the journey, and that's where I win!

So don't fret about mapping, or charts on the wall,
Let laughter be your compass, and you can't go wrong at all!

A Horizon of Hope

There's a horizon painted bright with dreams,
Where hope plays hide and seek in sunbeams.
I scale the mountains of popcorn and cheer,
Cracking up clowns who gather near!

With every sunrise, I melt like a tease,
Embracing the whimsy, just doing it with ease.
The clouds pass by, like frolicking bears,
And I giggle aloud without any cares!

I toss my worries into the vast sky,
Like confetti at birthdays that float and fly.
The horizon's alive, filled with laughter and hope,
A playful reminder help's all that you cope!

So lift up your spirits, let joy take the lead,
With a grin as your compass, we'll all take heed.
For on this great journey, filled with delight,
Hope's a horizon that makes everything bright!

The Mirror of Intentions

In the mirror, what do I see?
A reflection of what could be!
With hair so wild and eyes so bright,
I ponder my dreams with all my might.

Intentions gleam like disco balls,
Twisting and turning down glittery halls.
But wait, is that lunch stuck in my teeth?
I laugh and embrace my silly belief.

Every goal feels like a dance,
I trip on my hopes but still take a chance.
With every misstep, I learn to groove,
Finding joy in every silly move.

So I'll strut my stuff with all my flair,
In this strange journey, I'm light as air.
For what's the point of taking it all?
I'll keep on laughing, I won't let me fall!

Flickers of Enlightenment

A light bulb pops, it sparks and glows,
But sometimes it flickers, and no one knows.
Is it wisdom or just a bad bulb?
I ponder my thoughts while I try to solve.

With candles melting in my mind's sweet space,
I giggle at wisdom's silly pace.
Questions swirl like confetti in air,
And answers hide like they don't even care.

One thought comes dressed in a clown's attire,
"Chase your dreams, or just chase fire!"
I trip on the punchline, laugh and stare,
Who knew enlightenment could be such a flair?

But in the chaos of this thought parade,
I find each flicker does not fade.
With joyful jumps, I dance through it all,
In this circus of life, I'll take a fall!

A Bucket of Stars

I found a bucket, big and wide,
Filled with stars and dreams inside.
I reached for one, it slipped away,
Now I'm stargazing every day.

Each sparkly wish is stitched with care,
But some just pop like fresh hot air.
I catch a star, it sparkles bright,
Then turns into a firefly at night!

My neighbors think I've lost my mind,
Chasing stars, it's one of a kind.
I fish for dreams like they're in a stream,
And find they float better in a scream.

With glitter on my face and in my hair,
I'll gather my stars without a care.
For in this wild and funny quest,
Every twinkle reminds me I'm blessed!

The Garden of Potential

In a garden lush, potential grows,
With weeds of doubt that nobody knows.
I plant my dreams, but oh dear me!
Is that a flower or a stubborn weed?

I water hopes, I prune with glee,
Then trip on a root, oh woe is me!
But laughter bursts from the dirt below,
As tomatoes dance and sunflowers glow.

The bees hum tunes of secret plans,
While I attempt my garden dance.
Some blooms wither, others sprout wide,
Each one tells a tale, some I won't hide.

So I'll dig and sow with spark and cheer,
In my funny garden, there's nothing to fear.
For every twist and turn I take,
Leads to a harvest I'll gladly make!

The Weight of a Feather

A feather floats, so light and free,
Yet somehow weighs down my big ol' knee.
I ponder deeply, what could it mean?
Perhaps I need to eat some green.

To chase the dreams that tickle my brain,
I stumble around, looking quite insane.
But laughter echoes through thick and thin,
Guess I'll just keep on letting it spin!

A hop, a skip, and a silly dance,
I trip on purpose, just for a chance.
To find the joy in every blunder,
If life's a game, I'm under the thunder!

So I'll pack my bags, and off I'll go,
In search of wisdom, don't you know?
But first a snack and a nap, that's key,
For wisdom is best served with tea!

The Heart's Mosaic

My heart is a puzzle, so bright and neat,
With pieces of laughter, and others of sweet.
Yet sometimes I find, a rogue piece appears,
A sliver of stress sneaking in with the cheers.

Collecting the fragments, oh what a sight,
A mix of emotions, both funny and bright.
A splash of confusion, a dash of delight,
With some awkward moments, like dancing at night.

I try to arrange them into a new plan,
But often they scatter, like grains of sand.
Yet somehow I smile at the chaos I see,
For life's a mosaic, imperfect and free!

So here's to the art of the heart's playful beat,
With all of its colors, both sour and sweet.
Each piece tells a story, each laugh is a thread,
I'll wear my odd puzzle like a crown on my head!

Embracing the Journey

With shoes untied, I'm ready to roll,
The universe whispers, "Hey, that's your goal!"
I leap into days with a grin that's wide,
Embracing the journey, no need to hide.

A detour here, a hop down there,
I may trip on rocks, but I don't despair.
A tumble, a giggle, I get back up,
Finding joy in the hiccups, like filling a cup!

My roadmap's a doodle, not straight on a line,
Each scribble I make is a story divine.
With friends by my side, all eager to play,
We'll turn all the bumps into a grand ballet!

So here's to the wandering, the laughter, the cheer,
To chasing the sunset and not shedding a tear.
With every misstep, I'll dance like a fool,
Embracing the journey, oh ain't it a jewel!

Mosaic of Intentions

We scatter wishes like confetti,
Trying to assemble a grand plan,
With each failed attempt so petty,
We just laugh and take it as we can.

Our dreams are like socks on a line,
Hanging in the breeze, mismatched styles,
We ponder, 'Is this truly fine?'
As each gust of wind brings us smiles.

Plans are like pizza—lots of toppings,
Some are weird, yet who might complain?
We slice through the chaos, not stopping,
And savor the mess while it's plain.

So here we are, a puzzling art,
With colors blending, bright and bold,
Let's stick together, not fall apart,
In this canvas of chaos, let's be gold.

Raindrops on Dreams

Like raindrops falling on a tin roof,
Our hopes bounce and dance in the air,
Each drip's a giggle, what's the proof?
We laugh, even in the damp despair.

Umbrellas pop like mushrooms at dawn,
We waddle through puddles, splash and play,
Life doesn't come with a rulebook drawn,
So we frolic like kids without delay.

Dreams slip and slide like soap in the bath,
Wobbly plots twist and turn in jest,
Yet through the giggles, there's a path,
Finding joy in the soggy quest.

So let the rain fall, let laughter ring,
With each splash, our spirits align,
For in this silliness, we sprout wings,
Soaked in whimsy, our dreams will shine.

Dance of the Infinite

Twirl around like socks on a line,
Embrace the hiccups and awkward steps,
In this dance, we seek the divine,
With joyful leaps and tiny preps.

The rhythm of life's a bumpy ride,
Two left feet but we stomp and sway,
We trip and fall, then stride with pride,
Shaking off blunders, come what may.

Partners change like a wobbly tune,
Sometimes it's giggles, sometimes a groan,
We whirl under the silly moon,
Finding meaning in the overthrown.

So here's to the dance, let's not take it hard,
With grace of a potato, we'll sway,
In this grand ball where quirks are starred,
We'll laugh through the nights—oh, what a play!

Finding Fireflies

In the dark, we chase a glowing flick,
Like children lost in a glowing maze,
With nets and jars, we play the trick,
Searching for sparks through the night haze.

Each twinkle chats, then disappears,
A game of hide and seek so grand,
We giggle through hopes and whispering fears,
In every flash, a promise, a brand.

Jars fill with laughter and fleeting dreams,
Each flash a lesson, silly yet neat,
In this playful dance, or so it seems,
We're collecting magic, not just heat.

So let's run wild until the dawn,
With fireflies guiding in the fun,
For every laugh, a new wish drawn,
At daybreak, we'll glow—not just on the run.

Lanterns in the Dark

In shadows we wander, a giddy parade,
Chasing our dreams, with no grand charade.
With lanterns of laughter, we light up the night,
Stumbling on giggles, oh what a sight!

We dance with confusion, a twist and a spin,
Finding our purpose, where do we begin?
The path may be crooked, a patchwork of fun,
But oh, what a journey—this race has begun!

With jokes and with jests, we navigate fate,
In a world that is wild, we just can't be late!
For every mishap brings wisdom, it seems,
As lanterns grow brighter, we're fueled by our dreams!

So here's to the chaos, the laughs, and the play,
We tiptoe through life, dancing all the way.
With lanterns in hand, we embrace the spark,
And celebrate joy in the depths of the dark!

Portraits of Passion

With splashes of color and brushes so bright,
We paint our existence, in day and in night.
Each stroke tells a story, some silly, some sweet,
A gallery of giggles, we're never discreet!

In frames of our laughter, we capture our quirks,
Like squirrels on caffeine, or dancing with jerks.
A portrait unfolds, of dreams bizarre and wild,
Each picture a giggle, like a mischievous child.

We sketch out our hopes with a wink in our eye,
Our canvases shimmer, as we reach for the sky.
With palettes of whimsy, we color our fate,
In portraits of passion, we find that it's great!

So let's hang our laughter on walls made of cheer,
In galleries grand, where the fun's always near.
Every silly mishap, each laugh we recall,
Builds masterpieces vibrant, hung boldly for all!

The Essence of Today

A sprinkle of chaos, a dash of delight,
We gather the moments, while avoiding a fright.
In the essence of now, we leap and we twirl,
Like a cat on a hot tin roof, we whirl!

Today's not a riddle, it's a game to be played,
With giggles and wiggles, we're happily swayed.
Each tick of the clock brings a chance to go wild,
In the essence of now, we're forever a child.

We dine on the present, it's slapstick and fun,
With humor as seasoning, we savor each pun.
The laughter we gather, it flavors the day,
In the essence of today, who'd have it the gray?

So let's soak up the sunshine, the giggles that flow,
In the essence of now, we find joy as we glow.
With playful expressions, and hearts oh so free,
Today's a whimsical feast, join in with glee!

Kaleidoscope of Aspirations

With visions twirling, a colorful spree,
We twist and we turn, to find who we'll be.
In this kaleidoscope dance, dreams shimmer and gleam,
As we juggle ambitions and cookies and cream!

Life's a mystery puzzle, a jigsaw gone mad,
But each funny piece, shows the joy that we add.
Through shades and through shapes, we giggle and sway,
In this madcap collection of hopes on display.

With every new twist, we scream with delight,
As aspirations burst forth in a glittering flight.
Like butterflies buzzing, each color we find,
In a kaleidoscope world, we're all intertwined!

So let's keep on spinning, while the laughter prevails,
In this whirl of dreams, let's set the sails.
With aspiration's laughter, we embrace the bizarre,
In a kaleidoscope of joy, that's who we are!

The Aliveness of Moments

Catch the sun with a spoon,
Laughing while the shadows swoon.
Dance with squirrels on a whim,
Chase the thoughts till they grow dim.

Eat the cake, it's never too late,
Count each laugh, it's truly first-rate.
Hop on clouds, paint them pink,
Life's a puzzle, missing a link.

Swing with joy, on a spider's thread,
Tickle your toes, until they're red.
Underneath the moon's bright glare,
Forget the grown-up, let's just dare.

In the mess, we find the gold,
A sprinkle of chaos, warmly bold.
When in doubt, just sing and giggle,
For life's a jest, a grand, wild wiggle!

Unfolding the Layers

Peel me an onion, not too thin,
Layers of funny where do I begin?
Tiers of laughter, tears of glee,
Open your heart, swing wide your tree.

Underneath the skin, there's a joke,
Wrapped in laughter, it's no hoax.
Tickle the truth, with a pun so sly,
Unraveling life, give it a try.

Like a burrito, piled high,
With beans of joy and salsa spry.
Roll with fun, let the flavors clash,
In a wrap of dreams, we make a splash.

In this circus of the ordinary,
We juggle moments, oh so merry!
Crack the code with a cheesy grin,
Life's a riddle, let the fun begin!

The Canvas of Choices

Paint your morning with neon cheer,
Mix the colors—blue, green, and beer.
Brush with whimsy, splash like a dream,
Doodle your path, let spontaneity beam.

Each choice a stroke on a canvas wide,
A wobbly dance, take a silly ride.
Turn mistakes into splashes and stains,
Artfully crafted from joy and pains.

Splatters of breakfast, jam on the floor,
Life's just a mess we can't ignore.
Choose the glitter and throw some confetti,
With laughter and mess, we're always ready!

In the gallery where giggles reside,
Hang your quirks, wear them with pride.
Life's a painting, so strange yet fine,
Draw it your way, hubble-bubble divine!

Dust of Dreams

Sneeze at the stardust, float on a whim,
Catch a few wishes, give them a trim.
Juggle your hopes with a smile so bright,
Sprinkle your dreams like confetti at night.

Dust bunnies under the bed have a dance,
They twirl and prance, in a funny romance.
Whisk them away with a laugh and a sweep,
For dreaming is digging, even in the deep.

Tumble through life with whimsy and glee,
Put on your glasses, so you can see.
Each grain a story, a giggle, a jest,
Crafting a tale, let humor be the best.

So here we stand on this pile of delight,
With dreams like balloons, oh what a sight!
Dust of laughter, sprinkle it true,
In this grand circus, the stars are all you!

The Map of the Heart

They say love's a treasure, oh what a find,
But I lost it all, I swear I'm not blind.
Following arrows that point to the snacks,
Turns out they lead to my ex's old tracks.

I chart out my feelings with crayons and flair,
But my compass just spins, like I just don't care.
X marks the spot where I buried my pride,
But I can't find a shovel, and my map's got a slide.

I'll sail on the seas of confusion and glee,
To find out the answer, whatever could be.
My heart's like a puzzle, with pieces awry,
Yet I'll still grab a donut, while giving it a try.

So here's to the quest, with giggles and grins,
Finding my fortune, through losses and wins.
With humor my compass, and fun as my chart,
Who knew this adventure would tickle my heart!

Shadows of Regret

I once had a plan, all neat and precise,
But I tripped on a banana, slick as nice rice.
Regrets popped like popcorn, all over the floor,
Counting them up makes me laugh even more!

I pondered my choices, like a wise herbal sage,
Then I noticed my socks, mismatched on the stage.
Each little mistake, like a dance with a clown,
But isn't it funny how we still mess around?

The shadows of yesteryear flicker and tease,
Like a cat in a sunbeam, oh won't you please!
Chasing after what could have, should have been,
While sipping my coffee with a dopey grin.

So here's to the blunders, my newfound best mates,
We'll laugh at the past, my oh-so-great fates.
For what's a few stumbles, a tumble or two,
When life hands you wobbly, danceable blues?

Harvesting Sunlight

In gardens of giggles, I plant little seeds,
Watering hope with the silliest deeds.
I chase down the rays like a sun-shiny fool,
Harvesting laughter, my ultimate tool.

Sunshine is fickle, but I'll take my chance,
With shades of absurdity, I'll twirl in a dance.
Tomatoes of joy pop right off the vine,
While carrots of chuckles grow juicy and fine.

In fields overflowing with silly delight,
I'll gather the moonbeams to shine through the night.
With each little giggle and whimsical grin,
I'll cook up a feast where the fun can begin.

So pass me the sunshine, let's cook up some cheer,
With laughter as seasoning, I'll spread it all year.
For harvesting sunlight is truly an art,
And I'll make it my mission, with a jovial heart!

Footprints in the Sand

On beaches of laughter, I stroll hand in hand,
Waving to waves that build castles of sand.
Each footprint I leave has a story to tell,
Like the time I tripped over my own shoelace hell.

The tide rolls in gently, erasing my track,
But I giggle aloud, never looking back.
For every slip-up is a chance to enjoy,
Like when my flip-flop became a beach toy.

Seagulls above squawk their wise, silly lore,
Like "Why wear one shoe? You could beach it with four!"

I dance with the sea, my heart all aglow,
Painting joyous footprints wherever I go.

So here on the shore, with sand in my hair,
I'll follow those seagulls without any care.
For footprints in sand fade, but smiles always last,
We'll laugh at the waves and forget all the past!

The Dance of Moments

In a world of goofy twists,
We juggle dreams like clumsy fists.
Each second laughs, a fleeting chance,
Join the funny, wacky dance.

With every stumble, we embrace,
The joy of tripping through the race.
Like jellybeans in a wild parade,
We flip and flop, no plans are made.

A tickle here, a giggle there,
Life winks and whispers, 'Catch the air!'
In silly hats and mismatched socks,
We frolic free like dancing clocks.

So twirl and spin, don't take it straight,
With laughter loud, we celebrate!
In moments odd, the truth will bloom,
That joy abides in every room.

A Symphony of Choices

Choices clash like pots and pans,
With serenades from squirrel bands.
A question mark or maybe two,
Which socks today? The green or blue?

A buffet of paths spills out a feast,
Pick what's funky, not the least.
With side-eye glances and guffawing glee,
We'll navigate through calamity!

The music swells, then goes offbeat,
As we dance in shoes too big for feet.
A riddle rolls like a wayward drum,
In each weird note, we find some fun.

So gather round this merry crew,
With each decision, we'll see it through!
In laughter sings the sweetest choice,
With every blunder, hear our voice!

Unraveled Paths

Winding trails of tangled threads,
Each twist and turn plays in our heads.
With maps of pizza, laughs, and cheer,
We may get lost – but have no fear!

Every wrong way sings a song,
In make-believe, we can't go wrong.
Socks on our hands, hats on our feet,
It's a circus act, a wild treat!

Finding answers in jumbled dice,
Each wrong turn adds some extra spice.
With giggles echoing through the night,
Our messy journeys can feel so right.

So untangle not, the threads are fine,
In every knot, a twist divine!
With silly grins, let's forge ahead,
On uncharted paths, we're never misled.

The Quest for Meaning

We search for gems in muddy pools,
While wearing crowns made out of stools.
Is it coffee, cake, or silly hats?
Or chasing after pesky cats?

Each quest we take is full of cheer,
With every question sparking fear.
What's it all for? The answer pines,
In pancakes stacked in crooked lines.

Dance with ducks, and sing with bees,
The meaning wobbles in the breeze.
Like juggling pickles on a ride,
We grab for joy, with arms open wide.

So here's the truth, as clear as day,
The quest is fun, come what may!
With laughter bubbling, we'll ignite,
The spark of joy, forever bright.

Moments in Time's Canvas

A banana peel on the floor,
Watch your step or you'll adore,
Falling with a shout and grin,
Life's a trip, let the fun begin!

Coffee spills on a white shirt,
Reminds you that joy can hurt,
Laugh it off, it's just a stain,
Time's a canvas, let's not complain!

Dance like no one's watching you,
Even if your moves are askew,
Each concern is just a pun,
Life's a show, let's have some fun!

A cat that slips in a box,
Finding treasures in shock,
Unwrap the joys, set them free,
In this art, you'll find the key!

The Journey Within

Pack your bags, forget the map,
Take a detour, have a nap,
The journey's more than just the goal,
Grab a snack, let's rock and roll!

Step into shoes that are too tight,
Waddle like a penguin, what a sight!
Dance with fears, and twirl with glee,
Embrace the odd—the wild spree!

Chasing dreams on a pogo stick,
Bouncing high, oh what a trick!
Landing softly on soft green grass,
The funny falls—they come to pass!

From fears that scream to laughter bright,
Every stumble sparks delight,
For within each twist or turn,
A spark ignites, a lesson learned!

Echoes of Meaning

Whispers in the wind do cheer,
Like a joke you've heard all year,
Life's a riddle wrapped in fun,
With punchlines when the day is done!

Socks that don't quite match each other,
A fashion sense like no other,
Embrace the quirks, don't try to fit,
Find joy in every little bit!

Collect the moments, stack them high,
Catch the laughter as it flies by,
Each echo rings with a sweet reply,
In this giggle fest, we'll never die!

A good joke told at the right time,
Can make the mundane turn sublime,
So laugh and roll in colors bright,
Transform the day into pure delight!

Threads of Destiny

Tangled yarn, oh what a mess,
Creating sweaters that we guess,
But every loop holds something grand,
In quirky ways, we take a stand!

Picking flowers, one by one,
Wishing for just a little fun,
Each bloom a thread in our design,
Pluck a petal, and love's divine!

Each thread we weave, a story told,
In colors bright, both brave and bold,
A stitch of laughter, a patch of dreams,
Together we mend, or so it seems!

So tug the strings, let chaos reign,
Through silly paths, never mundane,
For in the fabric of each day,
We find the joy in every way!

The Secret of the Compass

In a world spinning round like a top,
You'd think I'd know, but I just can't stop.
North, south, east, or west, where to go?
I'll follow the cat; she seems to know!

With a compass that's broken, I'll make my way,
Chasing my shadow, oh what a play!
The stars above giggle, giving me clues,
While I trip over bushes and hop like a muse.

My compass, a buddy, just spins in delight,
Laughing at me in the quiet of night.
In circles I wander, forever lost
But I can't help it, I love at all cost!

So when I'm confused, I don't lose my cheer,
I dance with the winds, drink life like a beer.
Adventure awaits, in this topsy-turvy mess—
Who needs a straight path when laughter's the best?

Currents of Consciousness

Riding the waves of thought, I glide,
On a surfboard made of dreams, I ride.
How can I focus? I drift like a leaf,
Caught in a current—oh dear, what a grief!

Pondering apples while munching on pear,
I contemplate socks and their ultimate pair.
Butterflies flutter with wisdom so sweet,
While my mind's busy counting all of my feet.

Life's a stream overflowing with whim,
I dive in headfirst, and this isn't a hymn!
Jellybeans float like wishes untold,
As I splash in the water, so carefree and bold.

Riding those currents, I giggle and sway,
Searching for meaning in the silliest way.
Each droplet a laughter, each wave a new spark,
I'm swimming in nonsense, somewhere in the dark!

Navigating Without a Map

With no map in hand, I trudge up the hill,
Rummaging through pockets, but they're all still.
Where's the detour? What's the next step?
Oh wait, look! A squirrel, dancing adept!

I wander with purpose, or so that I claim,
Chasing my thoughts like a moth to the flame.
The trees whisper secrets, but I can't quite hear,
So I dance with the leaves, give a chuckle and cheer.

Improv is the motto, my fate in the mist,
Lost in the woods but not getting twisted.
A map would be handy, sure, it's no fuss,
But isn't it funny how I find the bus?

With no road to follow, I take to the skies,
I'm circling the sun with big, goofy eyes.
Who needs navigation when laughter's the key?
I'll wing it through life, just silly ol' me!

Dancing in the Rain

Umbrella in hand, oh what a mistake,
I throw it away for a big, goofy quake.
Dancing and splashing, twirling about,
While the world watches on with a giggling shout.

Raindrops are giggles falling from the sky,
Tickling my nose as I wiggle to fly.
Puddles like mirrors reflecting my glee,
I'm a wet little creature, wild and free!

Why seek the sunshine when storms bring delight?
Grinning in chaos feels oh-so right.
The clouds join my rhythm, a symphonic croon,
As I cha-cha my way under the bright silver moon.

Let the rain pour down, let it wash me anew,
As I laugh in the downpour, singing my tune.
Each drop a reminder to dance on the way—
With every storm's laughter, I celebrate the day!

The Magic of Now

Tick-tock, it's time to play,
Let's juggle our dreams today.
Past is foggy, future's vague,
Here's a snack, let's stop to wag.

Boredom's gone, we dance in glee,
Chasing squirrels, you and me.
Forget the goals, we twist and shout,
In this moment, there's no doubt!

Life's a ride on a bicycle,
Pedaling fast, it's quite a thrill.
We might fall or knock a cone,
But oh, the laughs we'll own!

Catch a breath, take a bow,
Let this laughter be our vow.
In the magic, we'll find the wow,
Together, let's embrace the now!

Flames of Aspiration

Chasing dreams like a firefly,
Catch one quick, oh my oh my!
Once it's caught, it slips away,
Time for cake? I'd rather play!

They say to climb the highest peak,
But I prefer my couch so sleek.
Goals are great, but so's a nap,
With popcorn snug upon my lap.

Set aflame those wishes bright,
But if they flicker, that's alright.
Some days are gold, some days are grey,
Can't I just eat a whole buffet?

The flames may dance; the embers glow,
Warming hearts, to them we go.
Through the chaos, come what may,
Let's shine our light in a funny way!

The Space Between

In the silence of in-betweens,
We find the strangest things it seems.
Like socks that vanish, quirks that clatter,
And thoughts like popcorn, oh what a scatter!

Between each word, a giggle springs,
And life's too short for serious flings.
So let's embrace the pauses tight,
Where laughter blooms and feels so right.

What's the rush? Just take a seat,
In the gap, there's fun to greet.
Life's a waltz, a jig, a hop,
In the space, the joy won't stop!

With each breath, we clear the air,
In gaps, we wiggle without a care.
Join the dance of the carefree scene,
In the space, we're all the queens!

Pedals on the Path

Pedals turn and wheels go round,
On this path of ups and downs.
With every bump, a silly squeal,
Steering straight, oh what a deal!

The destination? Who knows, my friend!
But let's ride 'til the tires bend.
We'll race the clouds, we'll dodge the trees,
Pedals thumping with the breeze.

The map's a mess, lost in delight,
But all this chaos feels so right.
With snacks on board and friends in tow,
We'll laugh and sing wherever we go!

So kick those pedals, let's not wait,
Adventure calls; oh isn't it great?
With silly hats and sunlight's wrath,
We find the joy upon our path!

Crystals of Wonder

In a world full of quirks and glee,
I searched for answers, not a tree.
With crystals that sparkled and danced,
I wondered if fate ever pranced.

A fortune told by a cat on a wall,
Said I'd find gold in the bathroom stall.
I laughed, oh what a silly old tale,
Yet, I still check for treasures without fail.

Balancing dreams on a spoon so frail,
I swirl round and round, oh what a trail!
The secrets of joy, tucked snug in my hat,
Who knew enlightenment lived with my cat?

With socks that don't match and hair like a fluff,
Who needs grand visions when life's just enough?
So here's to the whims that make us all smile,
With crystals of wonder, we'll laugh all the while.

Embracing the Unknown

I tiptoe into the void, oh so wide,
With donuts and sprinkles, I take it in stride.
With a wink and a chuckle, I face the strange,
How boring is safety? I've got to arrange!

The path may be foggy with no signs in sight,
Yet, I'll dance through the mist with pure delight.
A chicken with dreams, I'll flap in the breeze,
Finding joy in the chaos, oh do as you please!

With slippers that squeak and a hat full of flair,
I'll embrace every wild twist and turn with a care.
Like a penguin on ice, I may slip and slide,
But the fun of the ride is my joyful guide.

So here's to the unknown, let's giggle and cheer,
Each leap of the silly brings the laughter near.
In the arms of the wild, we'll shout, "Bravo!"
For life is a stage, and we're the main show!

Ripples of Intent

I tossed a penny in the pond today,
Hoping my wishes would splash and sway.
What a chaos of ripples, oh what a fund,
A fish made a face—was that my good pun?

With dreams that float like a paper boat,
I set them to sail, oh look, they just gloat!
Each wish makes a wave, some larger, some small,
I laughed as they danced, those dreams had a ball.

Like ducks in a row with a wobble or two,
My bright aspirations quacked loudly for you.
A champagne bubble wishes to grow,
But don't let them pop; let the laughter flow!

So here's to the ripples, let's shake up the pond,
With starlit ambitions, we're all a bit conned.
With giggles and grins, we'll float and delight,
In this bubbly escapade, everything's right!

The Tapestry of Time

In a tapestry woven with threads of surprise,
Each loop tells a story, oh what a rise!
A sock that went missing, a sandwich left plain,
Every stitch adds to laughter, not just the pain.

With yarn balls of memories all tangled in fun,
Like cats on a mission when they choose to run.
What a colorful mess, this fabric of fate,
I chuckle at timelines, oh isn't it great?

The clock may tick on with a funny old chime,
But who cares for worries? Let's dance out of time!
With quirks and oddities stitched in each seam,
We'll all wear our laughter, a whimsical dream.

So grab your knitting needles, come join me in rhyme,
Let's weave together this goofball design.
With a wink and a nod, we'll embrace the sublime,
In the tapestry of giggles, we'll laugh through all time!

www.ingramcontent.com/pod-product-compliance
Lightning Source LLC
Chambersburg PA
CBHW051630160426
43209CB00004B/594